what a WASTE!

WHERE DOES GARBAGE GO?

by CLAIRE EAMER

illustrations by BAMBI EDLUND

annick press
toronto + berkeley + vancouver

Edited by Linda Pruessen
Designed by Bambi Edlund

Annick Press Ltd.

We acknowledge the support of the Canada Council for the Arts and the Ontario Arts Council, and the participation of the Government of Canada/la participation du gouvernement du Canada for our publishing activities.

ONTARIO ARTS COUNCIL
CONSEIL DES ARTS DE L'ONTARIO
an Ontario government agency
un organisme du gouvernement de l'Ontario

Library and Archives Canada Cataloging in Publication

Eamer, Claire, 1947–, author
    What a waste! : where does garbage go? / Claire Eamer ; illustrated by Bambi Edlund.

Includes bibliographical references and index.
Issued in print and electronic formats.
ISBN 978-1-55451-918-7 (paperback).—ISBN 978-1-55451-919-4 (hardback).—ISBN 978-1-55451-920-0 (html).—ISBN 978-1-55451-921-7 (pdf)

1. Refuse and refuse disposal—Juvenile literature.
I. Edlund, Bambi, illustrator II. Title.

TD792.E26 2017   j363.72'88   C2016-906710-6
                                   C2016-906711-4

Distributed in Canada by University of Toronto Press.
Published in the U.S.A. by Annick Press (U.S.) Ltd.
Distributed in the U.S.A. by Publishers Group West.

Printed in China.

Visit us at annickpress.com.
Visit Claire Eamer at claireeamer.com.
Visit illustrator Bambi Edlund at bambiedlund.com.

Also available in e-book format. Please visit annickpress.com/ebooks/ for more details.
Or scan

With thanks to Alan Daley for the research help, smart ideas, meals at all hours, and generally for just being there—C.E.

For Ed Donlund—B.E.

CONTENTS

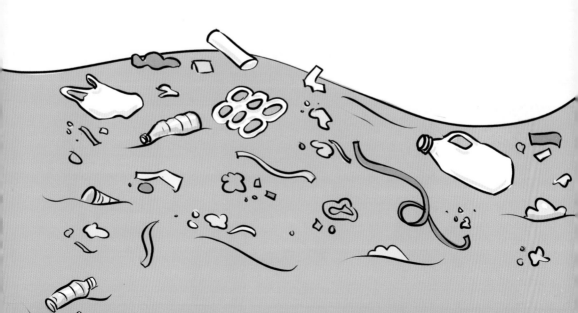

what is GARB

GARBAGE

SOON-TO-BE GARBAGE

GARBAGE

GARBAGE

GARBAGE

Simple question, right?

Garbage is just stuff you don't want and don't need. It's no good anymore, so you throw it away.

You might toss it in the garbage can or the recycling box or the compost bin or the dumpster in the alley. You might flush it down the drain or drop it on the ground. But those are just the first steps in throwing something away.

So, here's another simple question. Where, exactly, is "away"? Where does your garbage go after you toss it?

Actually, those two questions aren't simple at all. In fact, tracking down the answers will take us on a journey through time and around the world—from a South African cave still littered with the broken shells of a seafood feast that happened 162,000 years ago to the very edge of space, where dead satellites and other bits of garbage are orbiting Earth. We'll discover a mountain made from discarded olive-oil containers, an ocean of plastic, and tons of poop at the top of the world.

There's NEWS in the GARBAGE

Believe it or not, garbage is fascinating stuff. Archaeologists *love* garbage. Pyramids, cathedrals, and ancient temples tell us how people of the past wanted to be remembered. But their garbage tells us how they really lived. To an expert, a pile of garbage is a newspaper waiting to be read.

Just look at what gets tossed away in your kitchen. That garbage says a lot about how and where your family shops, what you eat, and how you prepare food. You'll probably find plenty of empty packages—cans and jars, boxes, cello- phane wrappers, plastic tubs from yogurt and ice cream, Styrofoam meat trays, and plastic bags. That's because most of us— in most parts of the world—shop at stores where food is packaged and ready to be stuffed into a grocery bag.

If your family lived a century ago, your kitchen garbage would have been quite different. The only packaging materials would have been cans, jars, bottles, and paper. No Styrofoam, cellophane, or plastic—those materials hadn't been invented yet or hadn't made it out of the science lab.

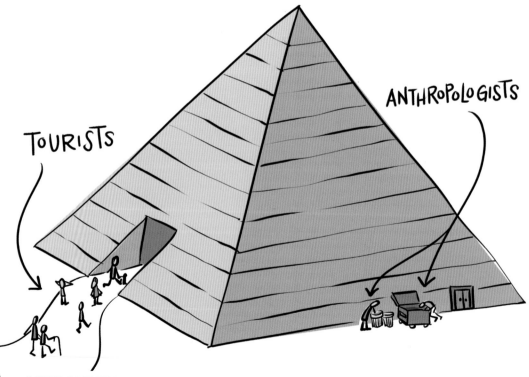

TOURISTS

ANTHROPOLOGISTS

And a century before that, in the early 1800s? Kitchen garbage was mainly bones and vegetable trimmings, with a few bits of broken glass or pottery. Cans wouldn't show up in the trash until canned condensed milk hit store shelves in the 1850s.

Those piles of kitchen garbage reveal how the people of the time lived, what they ate, how they prepared their food, and what kinds of materials were available to them. And each pile probably ended up in a different "away." That information, too, is part of the story garbage tells.

Garbage doesn't just tell a story. Today, it *is* a story. The news is full of reports about garbage: contaminated water spilling into streams, shiploads of old electronics abandoned in distant ports, discarded fishing nets entangling whales, cities running out of space to dump their waste.

Why spend so much time talking about trash? Well, the truth is that we produce a lot of it. In 2015, the United Nations Environment Programme estimated the total amount of solid waste produced around the world in a single year at 7 to 10 billion metric tons. That includes everything from trashed cars to stale bagels—all of it thrown away. It's a huge number, almost too big to imagine.

TrashTalk

Garbage · Trash
Rubbish · Waste
Litter · Refuse

All of these words mean
stuff you throw away.
But people use different words
in different parts of the world.
Which one do you use?

Try thinking of it in terms of polar bears. The biggest polar bear ever recorded—a shambling giant shot in Alaska in 1960—weighed about 1,000 kilograms (2,205 pounds), or 1 metric ton. So that annual pile of garbage is the equivalent of 7 to 10 billion giant polar bears. The line of bears, standing nose to tail, would reach to the moon and back at least 27 times.

No wonder garbage is in the news!

Dustbin
Garbage can
Trashcan
Dumpster
Rubbish bin

All of these terms mean a
container for waste. What's it
called in your neighborhood?

BAD NEWS, GOOD NEWS

People have always produced garbage. It's just part of living. You can't eat a clam supper—as those African diners did 162,000 years ago—without leaving a pile of clamshells. It would be like eating a plateful of chicken wings and leaving no bones. Today, however, humans are producing different kinds of garbage, and more of it than we have space for. We're running out of "away."

How did we get into this mess? Why is there so much garbage? Are some kinds worse than others? What is all of this trash doing to us and to the world? We'll explore all of those questions, and others too. An especially important one is whether there's still time to make a change.

The answer to that last question, fortunately, is a definite *yes!* In the pages that follow, we'll meet smart people with smart ideas—grown-ups and kids—and the governments and corporations that are supporting their efforts or coming up with their own. We'll encounter a Canadian man who started the blue box recycling movement and a Dutch teenager whose invention could help remove plastic from the world's oceans. We'll see how some companies are working together to cut down on the waste they produce, and how some governments are turning waste into energy—and money.

It's all part of the story of garbage—a story that's even older than we are.

CHAPTER 1

THE BEGINNING OF GARBAGE

Humans are really good at making garbage. We've been doing it for a long time—pretty much as long as there have been humans.

Our ancient relatives left garbage behind even before our own kind of human, *Homo sapiens*, arrived on the scene. About a million years ago, some of those relatives—probably members of a species called *Homo erectus*—sat around a fire in a huge cave in southern Africa. All that's left in the cave today is a layer of ash, but that ash includes the burnt remains of twigs and leaves that were probably used as fuel for the fire. It also contains bits of animal bones that

had been heated to temperatures you would expect from a small twig fire. It's hard to be sure after all this time, but it looks as if our ancient relatives might have been cooking dinner—the earliest evidence so far of cooking with fire.

Somewhat later—well, actually about half a million years later—some folks (more *Homo erectus*, since our species still hadn't shown up on the evolutionary tree) were sitting beside a quiet river in what is now Indonesia. We know this because they left a scattering of shells behind. Those shells tell us what those long-ago people were doing: collecting and eating freshwater mussels.

a WHOLE LOT of GARBAGE

Sure, that's garbage, but it's not garbage like we produce it, right? It's not mounds and piles and mountains of garbage. And it's biodegradable: it's all materials, such as wood, bone, and shell, that will eventually break down and disappear into the soil (although those half-million-year-old mussel shells haven't disappeared yet!).

Well, even biodegradable garbage mounts up. Remember those clamshells from 162,000 years ago? They've been traced back to a handful of people (*Homo sapiens*, this time) who sheltered in a large cave on the seashore near the southern tip of Africa. It was a great place to gather shellfish, enough for a small feast. The people pried the shells open, ate the contents, and left the shells behind, scattered on the cave floor. The pickings were so good near that cave that they kept coming back—and so did their children and their children's children. So many yummy shellfish meals were eventually eaten in that cave—over tens of thousands of years—that parts of the cave floor are now piled more than knee-deep with broken shells.

In other parts of the world, people tossed their garbage into piles instead of scattering it. The Florida Everglades, mostly a vast and soggy wetland, is dotted with green bumps—small islands that rise above the marsh and provide the perfect place for land-loving bushes and trees to take root. In fact, they are commonly called tree islands. For a long time, people thought the tree islands were odd geological formations. Recently, however, scientists have dug a little deeper. Literally.

Archaeologists excavated a few islands and discovered that they are actually rubbish heaps. About 5,000 years ago, the people who lived in the Everglades piled up bones, shells, scraps of food, charcoal from their fires, broken pots and tools, and anything else they didn't need. The decomposing food waste and other organic material fed plants, which grew in and over the mounds of rubbish.

Gradually, soil accumulated, and bigger plants flourished. Now the roots of trees keep the old garbage from washing away. Birds nest on the islands, and panthers and alligators take shelter there. Long-abandoned garbage has become an important part of the Everglades landscape.

Mudlark

In 19th-century London, mudlarks were children who waded barefoot through the mud of the River Thames, searching for rags, bits of metal, or anything else they could sell to buy food. In those days, the Thames was thick with garbage, raw sewage, and even rotting corpses, so it was a nasty and dangerous job.

A SIGN OF CHANGE

It's not only garbage itself that tells a tale. The way we get rid of garbage says plenty about us too. If archaeologists want to know whether an ancient site was a temporary camp or a place where people lived all year, they look for the garbage.

In a temporary camp, used for maybe a few weeks during fishing season or berry-picking time, people might leave garbage almost anywhere. Mostly, that garbage would be the same kinds of things found in the Everglades tree islands—food scraps, broken tools, maybe the sticks used for hanging fish to dry or a sheet of bark used as a berry bowl. By the time the people came back the next year, most of the garbage would be gone, scavenged by animals or dried up and blown away.

If you live in a place year-round, getting rid of garbage is a bigger problem. You can't just walk away from it, and the garbage isn't going to walk away either. When you throw something out, it has to go somewhere.

And that's what archaeologists look for—the somewhere, the "away" place, that tells them that people were living in a settlement long enough to have a garbage problem.

For those of us accustomed to carefully labeled trashcans that tell us what to throw out where, the places our ancestors chose to dump their garbage might be surprising. Early peoples often believed in the "out of sight is out of mind" approach. Rubbish might be dropped on the floor and covered with layers of dirt and fresh reeds or other greenery. Sometimes it was tossed into an unused room or shoved into an empty house. Often, household garbage was simply thrown into the street.

Rats love garbage, but people don't love rats. In the 19th century, you could make a living by catching and killing rats. In London, you could collect double pay by catching the rat alive (and getting paid by the homeowner) and then selling it to a local pub. In some pubs, watching dogs chase and kill rats was a popular form of entertainment.

Of course, throwing rubbish into the street doesn't make it go away. It does, however, change the street. If you keep tossing garbage out the window or the front door, perhaps covering it with dirt or just letting the rain and traffic pack it down, the street level will get higher. And higher. Add in the rubble from ruined buildings, broken bits of furniture, the sweepings from stables, and all the other junk generated by cities, old and new, and serious changes are likely to happen. Archaeologists calculate that in the ancient city of Troy, in what is now Turkey, the ground level rose at a rate of more than a meter a century over the 4,000 years of the city's history. That's a total of 40 meters (131 feet), or roughly the height of a 12-story building. The culprit? Garbage.

BURIED TREASURE

Sometimes, though, trash can be an unexpected treasure. Take, for example, an old rubbish pile in the Roman army camp at Vindolanda in northern England. About 1,800 years ago, people began dumping garbage near the corner of the commander's house. Occasionally, someone would throw some dirt or branches on the pile—maybe to keep the smell down—and then throw more stuff on top. It also got rained on. Northern England gets lots of rain!

Eventually, the house was torn down and other buildings rose on the site, covering the garbage and squashing it down. After centuries, the rubbish pile was buried deep under soil and rubble and soaked in water. In 1973, archaeologists drained the water from a deep trench so they could examine the layer of black muck at its bottom. It was that long-forgotten garbage heap.

As the archaeologists carefully teased apart the squashed layers of black gunk, they made an amazing discovery: hundreds of thin wooden tablets covered with writing. They had been protected from rot by being tightly packed together and covered with water—so well protected, in fact, that most of them were still readable.

These weren't ancient works of literature or great historical documents. They were notes from everyday life—lists of supplies; information about where soldiers were stationed; personal notes from soldiers and their wives; even an invitation to a birthday party. The first tablet the archaeologists found listed the contents of some long-dead soldier's care package from home—including several pairs of socks, two pairs of sandals, and two sets of underpants.

Knowing that people from so long ago invited their friends to birthday parties and sent gifts of warm socks and underwear makes them feel real to us in a way that no book of poetry or dry recital of history can match. A lot of what we know about the past actually comes from garbage.

Trash Talk

Midden

A polite archaeological term for a garbage pile—whether it's the remains of one family's household garbage or a huge pile of shells left by generations. Archaeologists love middens!

MIDDEN ↓

MODERN MIDDEN ↓

↑ HIDDEN MIDDEN

↑ SLID IN MIDDEN

SMART IDEA

The Stone Walls of Malta

Malta is a small island nation in the middle of the Mediterranean Sea. It has lots of sun, lots of rock, lots of historic buildings, and lots of ruins, going back at least 5,000 years.

It doesn't, however, have lots of land or wood. Farmers' small fields have to be fenced off to stop animals eating the crops. There's not enough wood to build fences, but plenty of stone. So the Maltese build stone walls. And they don't even have to dig up stone. After 5,000 years of buildings being raised up and knocked down, there's plenty of stone rubbish lying around.

If you look closely at a Maltese wall, you're likely to see the corner of a Roman column, a broken gravestone, a few rough-cut stone blocks from a medieval house, a finely worked block that might have come from a palace, and shattered rubble from World War II bombing raids. One Maltese farmer has even stuck a white ceramic toilet in among the stones of the wall bordering his field.

TOO MUCH of a BAD THING

For hundreds of thousands of years, we got away with tossing our garbage on the ground and walking away, or dumping it in the street and walking around it. But eventually, there was too much to ignore. Something had to be done. That time came sooner in some parts of the world than in others.

The Minoan people on the Mediterranean island of Crete decided to do something about their garbage around 3000 BCE. They dug large holes, dumped the refuse in them, and covered it, from time to time, with layers of dirt.

The ancient cities of Moenjodaro and Harappa went a giant step beyond Crete. They were built around 2500 BCE in what is now Pakistan. Many homes had built-in rubbish chutes and outside garbage bins. We don't know if they had organized systems for emptying the garbage bins and moving the waste out of the cities, because both cities were abandoned long ago—about 1900 BCE. Their ruins were rediscovered in the 20th century, and archaeologists are still trying to unlock their mysteries. But we do know that their waste disposal systems appear to be far more advanced than any others of the time.

In western Europe, the first official city dump was established outside the Greek city of Athens around 500 BCE. At the same time, the city government tried to clean up the streets by making it an offense to dispose of garbage less than a mile outside the city walls. Unfortunately, that rule didn't work very well. Walking half an hour each way to dump the day's waste was too inconvenient. Pretty soon, most people went back to dumping their garbage in the street.

archaeologists
(they study prehistoric humans and their tools)

epidemiologist
(he studies diseases)

I study the flavor of garbage!

GARBOLOGIST

OLOGIST CONVENTION

paleontologist
(he studies fossils)

anthropologist
(she studies humans, past and present)

The Street is Not Enough

So garbage is a mine of information for archaeologists, paleontologists, epidemiologists, anthropologists—and a whole range of other "ologists." But it's also a nuisance—and dangerous. Garbage attracts insects, rats, and other animals that gobble up good food as well as bad, and spread disease. It pollutes water. It's a breeding ground for germs of all kinds. And it smells terrible.

And today, we make a lot of it. Even small towns create more garbage than would fit in a rubbish pile at the corner of the commander's house or in a whole street of empty houses. On average, North Americans produce more than 2 kilograms (about 4.5 pounds) of waste every day. North America leads the waste-producing pack, but other regions are closing the gap fast. Coming up next: how we became superproducers of garbage.

CHAPTER 2

GARBAGE EXPLOSION

How did we change from a world in which people could just toss their trash into the streets to a world that produces dangerous—and ever-growing—amounts of waste?

In part, it's because of a population explosion. As of 2016, the global population was 7.3 billion—and growing. The United Nations estimates it will hit 9.7 billion by 2050. It's hard to picture how big that number is, but consider this:

historians' best guess for how many people were alive in 2500 BCE, when Moenjodaro was founded, is roughly 25 million. That means for every single person alive in Moenjodaro's time, there are 300 people alive today.

Think about how much garbage one person can create. Now multiply that by 300. That's part of the reason for the garbage explosion. But it's not the whole story.

COUNTRY GARBAGE, CITY GARBAGE

How many people there are is important, but so is *where* those people are. The scientists who prepared a 2012 report on waste for the World Bank estimated that people who live in cities create at least twice as much garbage as people who live in the country. And more and more of us are city people. In 1900, most people in the world still lived in the country or in very small communities. Only 13 of every 100 lived in cities. A century later, 49 of every 100 people lived in cities—almost half the world's population.

It's not that city people are extra messy. They just live differently from country people. In most of the world, people who live in the country grow some of their own food and buy some from a neighbor or a local store. Their food waste probably goes into a compost pile to fertilize crops or the garden. They might sew their own clothes and even make their own cloth. In the developed world, where city conveniences such as grocery and clothing stores are often available to country people too, garbage production is still usually lower in the country. It's not quite so easy to pop into a coffee shop for a drink in a disposable cup or to stop at the corner store for a bag of chips when both the coffee shop and the corner store are a 20-minute drive away. And you're likely to think twice about taking home the disposable cup and the chip bag when you and your family have to haul the garbage to the dump yourselves.

In the city, people work in factories and offices and stores. They go home at night to apartments or houses with small yards. They usually don't have time or space to grow their own food, so they buy food from stores. They buy ready-made clothes, drinks in throwaway bottles, and lunches in takeout containers. All of that activity creates garbage, and someone else usually collects the garbage and carts it away. Out of sight is out of mind.

The stores, factories, offices, and activities that draw people to the city produce garbage too, and so do all the transportation systems that bring food and goods to city stores. And then, of course, there's pee, poop, and other fairly disgusting things that people and animals produce every day. That stuff needs to be disposed of too. In the country, at least some of it becomes manure to fertilize fields and gardens, but manure (and the smell that goes with it) isn't popular in the city!

So—more city folk means more garbage. But that still isn't the whole story.

UPPER GULLYFLUFF

LOWER GULLYFLUFF

Gullyfluff

A 19th-century American word for the grungy crumbs, dirt, and other bits of waste that accumulate in your pockets.

Pure

Dog poop. In London in the 19th century, a "pure finder" was a person who collected dog droppings from the streets and sold the stuff to tanners, who used it to cure leather.

SMART IDEA

Don't Toss It. Fix It!

Have your favorite shoes sprung a leak? Is the toaster setting off smoke alarms? Does your computer screen flicker? Take them to a Repair Café! The first Repair Café opened in Amsterdam in October 2009. Five years later, there were more than 750 Repair Cafés in at least 17 countries. There might be one near you.

A Repair Café is an event more than a location. It happens whenever and wherever people organize it. In Santiago, Chile, the Repair Café takes place in a community marketplace located around an old train station. In Dublin, Ireland, it happens in a church hall. In Zushi, Japan, it's part of the annual Zushi Environment Festival.

Repair Café volunteers provide refreshments and tools, set up work areas, and supply repair manuals and information about waste reduction. People who have things to repair show up, and so do people who know how to fix them. You can learn how to mend your shoe, repair the toaster, or figure out what's wrong with the computer. Or you can just hang out and exchange smart ideas.

REPAIR CAFÉ today!

LET THE GOOD TIMES ROLL

Between 1950 and 1970, the population of the United States grew by almost a third, but the amount of garbage Americans created grew twice as fast. Cities were growing, but even that didn't account for the explosion of garbage. Something else was happening—prosperity.

Up until the late 1940s, the 20th century had been pretty tough on most of the world. World War I, the Great Depression, and then World War II left most people with little money to spare. But in the 1950s, times got better—particularly in the United States.

There were plenty of good-paying jobs. Many people found that they could pay for food, housing, and all the other basics and still have money left over. So they bought extras: things (such as washing machines, cars, and prepared foods) that made life easier and other things (such as television sets, nice clothes, and toys) that made life more fun. Manufacturers were happy to produce these extras, and stores were happy to sell them. And advertisers were happy to convince people they actually needed all of those things—that buying more stuff would make *them* happy too.

So people in the U.S. bought more, used more, broke more, and threw away more. And over the last few decades, country after country has followed the same path—growing cities, growing prosperity, growing garbage.

The THROWAWAY Message

There's yet another reason for the garbage explosion. Today, we actually make garbage on purpose.

Think of plastic toys, music players, batteries, even pens and markers. When they break or wear out, they can't be fixed. They aren't meant to be. All you can do is toss them in the garbage.

SMART PERSON

The Blue Box Man

The symbol of recycling for millions of people in North America, Europe, New Zealand, and Australia is the blue box. It might be big or small or even a wheelie bin, but if it's blue, you know that's where the recycling goes for curbside pickup.

It all started with one enthusiastic Canadian recycler. In the 1970s, Toronto resident Jack McGinnis felt so strongly about reducing garbage that he'd take his neighbors' cans and bottles to the recycling depot along with his own. He was happy to do it, but he knew that getting people to do their own recycling would be even better. McGinnis figured the answer was to make recycling convenient. There would have to be a curbside pickup service, just like the municipal garbage service. And there had to be a way to identify the recyclable stuff easily. So he designed a plastic box, marked with a logo and the proud boast "We Recycle."

McGinnis founded the Recycling Council of Ontario in 1978. Three years later, he helped organize the first experimental blue box collection program in Kitchener, Ontario. It worked. Soon other Ontario communities jumped on board. By the time Jack McGinnis died in 2011, the blue box program had spread around the world and greatly increased people's awareness of the importance of recycling.

And why are the boxes blue? Plastic gradually breaks down in the sun and rain, but blue plastic survives longer than any other color.

Others items become obsolete and useless long before they break. A computer manufactured 20 years ago might still work, but if it can't use modern programs or connect to modern devices, it's garbage.

And all of these disposable items come with another kind of garbage: packaging. The memory card for your computer or camera might be the size of your thumbnail, but it comes packaged in paper and plastic as big as a book. Ready-made lunches are sold in plastic containers, accompanied by plastic spoons and disposable packets of sauce or dip—almost as much packaging as food.

For many countries, this is a recent development. China didn't have a packaging problem until 1981. That's when the country's first supermarket opened. Before that, there were no stores where everything is packaged and set out on shelves for customers to pick up. Instead, people told store clerks what they wanted, and the clerks handed over the items— wrapped, at most, in a bit of paper. City garbage was mostly food scraps and other biological waste that was trucked to the country for fertilizer or methane gas production. But China has become prosperous over the last few decades. Now it has big stores with shelves full of things to purchase. People are buying more packaged goods every year, and the throwaway material is turning into mountains of garbage. Today, China, with about one-fifth of the world's population, produces almost one-third of the world's household waste.

In 2010, the Chinese government passed the world's first law against excessive packaging to try to slow down the growth of garbage. The situation was urgent: Chinese cities were running out of space to get rid of garbage. They weren't alone.

the ITTY BITTY Tiny Card

The heavy plastic and cardboard packaging that typically surrounds a digital memory stick or card can be 15 times larger than the product itself.

CHAPTER 3

DOWN
IN THE
DUMPS

Today, China and many other countries are struggling to find solutions to an all-too-common problem: where to stash the trash. For centuries, dumps have been the most popular answer. In Central America more than 1,000 years ago, the Mayans even had separate dumps for organic waste—like food scraps—and inorganic waste, which mostly came from workshops that manufactured things like obsidian tools. The inorganic waste, such as stones and broken pottery, was hauled to building sites in the city to be used as fill in walls and foundations.

Once you have a dump, the next problem is convincing people to use it. Since dumps are smelly and messy, they're generally located well away from where people live. That means transporting the garbage all the way to the dump. How do you convince

people to make the effort? Just passing a law didn't work in Athens. Other places tried hiring people to do the work. Eventually, most cities had garbage collectors of some sort— often people who made a living by collecting and picking through other people's discards.

But having a dump and somebody to deliver the garbage to it still doesn't solve all the waste problems.

TRASH BITES BACK

At its simplest, a dump is a big hole in the ground. You put garbage in and cover it up, from time to time, with a layer of dirt to keep the smells down and the scavenging animals out. And then you repeat until full. That's still the way garbage is handled in much of the world.

Dumps are certainly an improvement over tossing garbage into the street, but they aren't perfect. Even if the garbage is covered with dirt periodically, it's still basically open to sun, wind, and rain, and to scavengers of all kinds. The garbage rots in the sun, blows around in the wind, and washes into streams and groundwater when it rains, polluting them with all kinds of unhealthy substances. Animals spread it around and then invade neighboring fields and houses in search of

even more food. They pick up diseases from the garbage and spread them to humans.

Dumps can also catch fire. In 2014, the dump in the small Arctic Canadian town of Iqaluit caught fire and burned for four months. The inferno reached a temperature of 2,000°C (3,632°F), about twice as hot as a blazing bonfire, and created so much smoke that schools were closed for days. The only way to put the fire out was to pick the garbage pile apart and dunk the burning trash in water, one bulldozer load at a time.

Dumps can even explode, sometimes with no warning. Rotting garbage releases explosive methane gas. If it collects in pockets in the dump, all that's needed is a spark to cause an explosion. Even the heat from the rotting garbage might be enough.

TIDYING the DUMP

In the 20th century, engineers designed a new and improved kind of dump called a sanitary landfill. A landfill might look like a regular dump, but it's a lot more complicated—and a lot more expensive.

A landfill usually starts as a giant hole, but the hole is lined with clay and plastic to make sure none of the garbage leaks into the ground and water beneath. Pipes collect rainwater and other liquids that seep through the garbage, picking up contaminants as they go. That liquid—called leachate—is pumped out and treated so that it's safe. Other pipes capture the gases (mostly methane) produced by the rotting garbage so that they too can be disposed of—without exploding or causing fires. Each day's garbage is covered with a layer of packed soil to keep scavengers out, keep the garbage in, and reduce the smell.

It sounds very tidy, but sanitary landfills have problems of their own. Even when landfills are as leakproof as technology can make them, it takes regular maintenance to keep them that way. And you can't just forget about them once they're full. Rain still falls and trickles through the layers, creating leachate, and the buried garbage still creates gases. Landfills have to be maintained long after that last load of garbage arrives.

Landfills also take up a lot of space. As more and more garbage arrives, the landfill grows, spreading wider and growing higher. The Puente Hills landfill near Los Angeles, California, operated for 56 years. By the time it closed in 2013, it was a large hill—about as high as a 55-story building—and it spread over enough land for a small

city. Now it's gradually being turned into a park, a job that will take years.

Across an ocean or two from Puente Hills is Ariel Sharon Park in Tel Aviv, Israel. It used to be a massive landfill called Hiriya Mountain. (The most polite translation of that name is *stinky hill!*) It closed in 1999 after 47 years of operation. In 2001, Israel began to turn its stinky hill into a huge ecological park. Now people walk, cycle, run, stroll past ponds, and admire the view from what was once a pile of garbage.

One of the biggest garbage dumps in the world is in Brasília, a large city in Brazil. In 2014, it covered an area equal to 194 football fields. And it's still growing.

EVERYTHING OLD IS NEW AGAIN

One way to solve the problem of giant dumps and landfills is to head off a lot of the garbage before it gets that far. Many cities now have recycling and composting programs that reduce the amount of garbage going into landfills, in some cases almost entirely. It's a new idea that isn't really new at all.

In the 18th and 19th centuries, the Industrial Revolution swept through Europe and North America. New machines in huge factories and mills could produce cheap goods in large quantities. People moved into cities to work in the factories, and—just like today—the cities grew. But the amount of garbage didn't increase at the same rate. Some rubbish was so valuable, in fact, that you could make a good living collecting it and reselling it. Rags were made into paper. Animal bones were turned into glue, grease, and chemicals used to make matches, refine sugar, and manufacture photographic materials. Tin cans became metal toys. Any kind of animal or vegetable material, from old shoes to potato peels, was hauled to the countryside and turned into fertilizer.

Lots of people still make a living by recycling trash. They're called waste pickers or ragpickers or—in Egypt—the Zabaleen. The Zabaleen have served as informal garbage collectors in the city of Cairo since the 1940s. They collect about two-thirds of Cairo's waste, going from door to door with donkey carts and pickup trucks and hauling the day's take back to their homes to sort. They sell what they can or make new goods from the recycled waste and sell them. Food scraps get fed to the pigs many Zabaleen keep in rooftop gardens. Most Egyptians are Muslim and don't eat pork, but most of the Zabaleen are Christian—so the pigs eventually become dinner. Altogether, about 85 percent of what the Zabaleen collect is recycled.

Trash Talk

WOBBLY CHAIRS

BEARS

MOSQUITOES

FLAT BIKE TIRES

Nuisance grounds

An old, mostly Canadian term for the municipal dump—where you throw all the stuff that's, well, a nuisance.

Disco rice

A slang term invented by New York City sanitation workers. It refers to the squirming maggots that thrive in many of the city's garbage dumpsters.

LANDFILL

NO VACANCY

Even with all the effort put into keeping stuff out of landfills, some cities have run out of places to put their garbage. New York City spends hundreds of millions of dollars each year to send its garbage well beyond the city limits. Every day, about 23,000 metric tons of garbage are loaded onto trains and trucks and carried to landfills as far as 500 kilometers (310 miles) away—

at least a six-hour drive. The city pays landfill owners well to take the garbage, but not everyone wants a giant landfill in their neighborhood, so it's tough to find new places for the constant stream of trash.

LANDFILL

Singapore has an even bigger problem. The island city in Southeast Asia is home to about 5.5 million people—and it has no spare land for garbage. Its only landfill is an artificial island called Pulau Semakau (Malay for Mangrove Island), built from incinerated garbage. In the 1990s, Singapore's growing prosperity brought the usual problem of growing piles of garbage, so the government began a campaign urging people to recycle. The country's waste disposal companies also recycle as much they can. Anything that remains is burned in huge incinerators, which provide about 3 percent of Singapore's electricity. The garbage ashes are dumped in plastic-lined cells on Pulau Semakau. Once the cells are full, they're covered with soil and planted with grass. A few trees have sprouted on the island, and mangroves flourish along the shoreline. People now come to watch birds and wander the beaches of an island made of garbage.

SMART PERSON

From Rags to Respect

Suman More has been collecting and sorting garbage in the streets of Pune, India, for more than 35 years. When she and her husband first moved to Pune, that was the only kind of work they could get. At first, she mainly collected scrap metal that she could sell for a little money. Later, she realized that sorting the scrap and other garbage first would earn her more money. Still, it wasn't much. Suman and her husband skipped one meal a day for years to make sure their four children could go to school.

A few years ago, the waste pickers of Pune formed an organization and negotiated an agreement with the municipality. Now they—and Suman—officially collect the city's garbage, sort it, and deliver it to processing centers. In return, they earn a decent salary. Today, Suman travels to international conferences to talk about the important work waste pickers do.

And her children? They're all grown up and married, at university, or working in good jobs. Suman still collects garbage, but now she uses her salary to send other poor kids from Pune's slums to school.

CHAPTER 4

A RECIPE FOR WASTE

Soggy lettuce. Moldy bread. Meat that's past its best-before date. In 2012, Americans threw away about 35 million metric tons of food. According to the U.S. Environmental Protection Agency, that's about one-fifth of everything thrown out that year, a larger fraction than any other kind of garbage, including plastic and paper. And the United States isn't alone. A recent study showed that European Union countries waste about 22 million metric tons of food each year.

In fact, between one-third and one-half of all the food produced in the world each year is wasted, according to the United Nations Food and Agriculture Organization. And when that food ends up in dumps and landfills, it's trouble. It attracts insects and other scavengers. It rots, giving off methane, a greenhouse gas that contributes to global warming.

But there's an even worse problem. Not all of that food needs to be wasted. Most of it could have been eaten, yet millions of people around the world go hungry every day. So why does so much food end up rotting in dumps and landfills?

FOOD for THOUGHT

Food gets thrown away for a lot of different reasons—and not always good ones. People toss out meat, cheese, yogurt, and all kinds of dairy products before the sell-by date marked on the package, just because it's getting close. Packaged salads and sandwiches from a store's ready-to-eat section are thrown out if they haven't been bought by the end of the day.

Food gets wasted just to make way for other food. Bread and other bakery products are trashed to make way for the next day's baking. Packaged food, such as soups and noodles, are tossed to make room for new shipments. Restaurants throw away unused prepared food at the end of the day because they have nowhere to store it and, often, are not permitted by law to keep it.

What Do Those Dates Mean?

Lots of foods have dates marked on the packaging. Here's what they mean:

- **Sell-By:** A guide for stores about how long they can display the product for sale. You should buy it before that date, but it will still be good to eat past that date.

- **Use-By, Best if Used By, Best By, Best Before:** Dates to tell you how long the product is likely to remain at its absolute best when unopened.

None of these labels mean that the food can't be eaten after the date on the package. If you store them properly, many kinds of food will still be good to eat for some time. The best guides to food quality are your senses. If the food looks, smells, or tastes a bit wrong, toss it.

THE UGLINESS FACTOR

Sometimes food is thrown out for reasons that make no sense. Would you throw away a potato because it was too ugly? Potatoes can be big or small, red or brown, round or oval. But beautiful? You don't usually look for beauty in a potato, so ugly shouldn't matter. But it does. The big grocery chains that sell most fruits and vegetables want only the pretty ones—the ones that look like the customer's picture of a perfect peach or an ideal potato.

For a vegetable, getting out of the field and into a store is like winning a beauty contest. The losers, the vegetables that aren't nearly perfect in every way, are often left to rot in the field or tossed straight into a landfill. In some parts of the world—North America, Europe, and Australia, for example—these unattractive left-behinds make up almost one-third of all fruits and vegetables grown.

Even if a potato makes it out of the field, there's no guarantee it will reach someone's belly. The next challenge is the grocery store shelf. Every day, stores around the world fill their produce shelves with fresh fruit and veggies. There are mountains of bright red tomatoes and shiny green apples, and bin upon bin of broccoli and bananas. And potatoes.

But is everything on those shelves bought by the end of the day? Not even close! Most storeowners refill their shelves throughout the day so shoppers don't feel that they're picking through the leftovers. At the end of the day, much of what's left on the produce shelves is tossed out.

Our potato might get lucky and make it into someone's grocery bag, but it's still not safely on the way to dinner. A 2015 study revealed that British households throw away almost 6 kilograms (13 pounds) of food each week. This is partly because of the way we shop. We buy what we think we're going to need, or we buy extra because there's a sale, or we buy things just because they look appealing—"Oh, look at that pretty potato!" And then we don't use them. The potato sits in the refrigerator, forgotten. Eventually someone reaches in and pulls out a shriveled lump with sprouts beginning to poke through its skin. And our poor potato, after a long and hazardous journey, is thrown away, still uneaten.

In 1840s New York City, pigs were garbage collectors. Free-roaming pigs wandered the city, eating whatever had been thrown into the street— meat, bones, rotting vegetables, scraps from inns and kitchens, anything. Eventually, the pigs were slaughtered and turned into pork, ham, and sausage. And the residents of New York City ate the pigs. Now that's recycling!

BEYOND GARBAGE

Reducing food waste would reduce our garbage problem. But it would also do a lot more. It costs a lot to produce food—in time, work, fertilizer, fuel, and water. Throwing food away without using it doesn't cut down on those costs. And rotting food is a major source of greenhouse gases. In 2013, the UN Food and Agriculture Organization estimated

SMART PERSON

Junk Food Man

Chef Adam Smith takes collecting and sharing waste food to the next level. In December 2013, he opened the Real Junk Food Project—a tiny café in Armley, a shabby community in northern England. You could load your plate with soups, salads, hot food, cold food, cupcakes, and fruit—and pay only what you felt like paying.

Too good to be true? Not really. All the food is rescued from the garbage bin—usually before it even gets there. It comes from grocery suppliers, supermarkets, bakeries, and restaurants. Every day, Smith and his army of helpers collect it, cook it up, and feed people. In its first 10 months,

the café fed 10,000 people, using 20 tons of discarded food.

The idea caught on fast. A year and a half after the first Real Junk Food café opened, there were more than two dozen similar pay-what-you-want cafés in Britain alone, and people from as far away as Brazil and Warsaw had contacted Smith for information about opening cafés in their cities.

that food wastage produces enough greenhouse gases to make it the world's third-top emitter, behind the United States and China.

That's all bad enough, but consider also the hundreds of thousands of people who could be fed by the food that is wasted every year. The United Nations estimates it's enough to feed 2 billion people. They also estimate that about 842 million people—fewer than half that number—suffer from hunger and need that food.

How is it possible that so many people can be hungry in a world that produces—and wastes—so much food? Sometimes, poor distribution is the problem: food just doesn't get to the people who need it. That makes sense if the people live on the other side of the world from where the food is produced, or in an area where transportation isn't reliable. But what about the hungry people who live just down the street or across town from the places where food is wasted? Often the problem is money. The food is there, but the people who need it don't have enough money to buy it.

People around the world have begun adding up the costs of food that goes into the garbage instead of to people who need it. And plenty of them are finding ways to fight back.

Trash Talk

Hog's-wash

In 19th-century England, people went from door to door collecting dishwater and cooking water, table scraps, spoiled food, sweepings from the floors of bakeries and public houses, and anything even slightly edible. The sloshing buckets of waste were fed to pigs, so they were called hog's-wash. Today, talking hogwash means talking rubbish!

Trencher

A plate made of stale bread, used by diners at feasts in medieval Europe. After the feast, the used trenchers, full of sauce and bits of food, might be given to dogs or handed out to the poor. No waste, and no dishwashing!

INGLORIOUS
fruits & vegetables

MAKING UGLY BEAUTIFUL

In 2014, the French super-market chain Supermarché decided to celebrate the ugly potato, the twisted carrot, and all the other fruits and veggies that failed the beauty test. The chain launched an "Inglorious Fruits and Vegetables" campaign, bought tons of ugly produce from their growers, cleared whole aisles of their stores to display them, and offered them at bargain prices.

The inglorious fruits and veggies were a glorious success. Not only did the produce sell—and quickly—but far more people than usual came to shop in the stores. If you're willing to put up with oddly shaped carrots and less-than-perfect apples, you can now buy them at bargain prices in at least half a dozen countries. A second French chain sells ugly fruits and vegetables as *Les Gueules Cassées* (Busted Faces). In Canada, they're called The Misfits or Naturally Imperfect. In Australia, they're The Odd Bunch or Imperfect Picks.

And the movement is spreading. Ugly fruits and veggies might be at a store near you. If they aren't, ask for them. That's how the movement started in the first place.

SMART IDEA

Gleaning

In February 2013, English farmer Geoff Philpott had a lot of cabbages and cauliflowers that no supermarket would buy. The cauliflowers weren't tightly bunched, and the outer leaves of the cabbages had been pecked by pigeons. They were good to eat, but they weren't pretty. So Philpott called in the Gleaning Network UK.

Gleaners were once a normal part of farming. They followed the people harvesting the crops and collected the fruits, vegetables, or grains the harvesters had missed. On modern farms, food still gets left in the field.

Harvesting machines miss it, or the fruits and vegetables aren't large enough or pretty enough, or there's more produce than the farmer can sell before it goes bad. Now gleaning is making a comeback.

Gleaning Network volunteers descended on Philpott's field and harvested two tons of cauliflowers and cabbages in a single day—about 25,000 servings of good, fresh veggies that all went to people in need. The Gleaning Network is part of a worldwide revival of gleaning, ranging from national networks to local groups that connect people who want fresh produce to local gardeners who have too much.

WASTED FOOD
IN HUNGRY LANDS

The food waste problem
goes well beyond big supermarkets
and wealthy countries. A 2014 United
Nations report pegged the food wastage rate in Latin America and the
Caribbean at about 15 percent, far less
than North America or Europe, but still
enough to feed all the hungry people in
that region.

In Africa, too, plenty of food is
wasted while plenty of people go
hungry. Nigeria is one of the world's
major producers of tomatoes, but almost
half the tomatoes harvested there are
spoiled or wasted before they ever get
to a store. The problem: poor harvesting
methods and a lack of reliable storage
and transportation systems.

In Kenya, it's the ugly vegetable
problem. Many Kenyan farms and
market gardens sell their produce to
European supermarkets, and up to a
third is rejected because of its appear-
ance. Unfortunately, the rejected
produce rarely makes it to hungry
Kenyans because of problems with
shipping and storing. In December
2014, hundreds of Kenyans fought
back with Africa's first Disco Soup,

part of an international movement
raising awareness of food waste. A
small army of volunteers collected
rejected produce from Kenyan
farms: too-small carrots, too-curvy
beans, chili peppers that were the
wrong color. They chopped, cooked,
and shared the food with local residents and street children during a
giant party.

CHAPTER 5

DOWN the DRAIN

The summer of 1858 was sweleringly hot in London—but the heat wasn't what people were talking about. It was the smell. The wide River Thames, which winds through the center of London on its way to the sea, smelled so bad that newspapers ran headlines about the summer of The Great Stink.

The problem was that the Thames served as London's sewer. A city of 3 million people creates a lot of sewage, and it was all rotting in the summer heat. And the Thames wasn't just a sewer. It was also London's main supply of water for washing, cooking, and drinking. That's a recipe for disaster.

COOL FACT

Attack of the Fatberg

Having a good sewer system isn't enough to get rid of the gunk. You have to keep it all flowing, and that isn't always easy. Meet the fatberg! It stinks, it's disgusting, it's really, really big—and it's clogging city sewers around the world.

A fatberg is a rotting mass of congealed fat and household waste.

In 2015, a 10-metric-ton fatberg as long as the space shuttle (40 meters, or 131 feet) blocked and broke the sewer beneath the London district of Chelsea, causing a very expensive two-month repair. A year earlier, a smaller fatberg threatened the sewer system in Melbourne, Australia. New York City alone has spent $18 million over five years dealing with the problem.

How do you get a fatberg? The main culprits are cooking oils and fats poured down the drain, and wet wipes, those premoistened cleanup tissues originally used for wiping babies' bums, but now marketed to adults too. Cooking oil might be liquid when it goes down the drain, but it soon turns into semisolid sludge, and wet wipes don't disintegrate like toilet paper. Instead, wipes and fat tangle in a giant, disgusting knot that just keeps growing. Other material can get caught up in the growing mass. A giant fatberg in England also contained rotting food, wood planks, and even *tennis balls*!

DANGEROUS WASTE

The stuff we get rid of in the dump or landfill is only part of the garbage story, and not even the smelliest part. That title probably goes to poop and pee and puke—or excrement and urine and vomit, if you want to be a bit more formal. Think about all the stuff that gets flushed down the toilet, washed down the sink, or sluiced into the storm drains in the street. And then think about that stuff pouring out of your kitchen tap. Beyond disgusting!

It's also beyond dangerous. Human waste can spread disease, so mixing sewage with the water supply is a really good way to make a lot of people very sick indeed. One of the nastiest diseases that can be spread by contaminated water is cholera, a horrible kind of diarrhea capable of killing its victims in hours. When people are sick with cholera, the germs come out with the diarrhea and get into the sewage. If that wastewater contaminates drinking water, even more people get sick.

In 1854, four years before The Great Stink, a cholera epidemic killed almost 11,000 Londoners in a matter of weeks. John Snow, a doctor who was determined to figure out how the disease spread, discovered that all the victims had used water from a single well contaminated by sewage from an open drain. He presented his findings to London authorities, but they weren't convinced and did nothing.

However, The Great Stink was too much for them to ignore. It was so awful that the city government finally began to build a sewage system to carry London's waste downstream, away from the city and its water supply. The project took about 10 years to complete, and involved the construction of almost 22,000 kilometers (13,670 miles) of pipes and channels—most of them still in use today.

To the surprise of London authorities, getting rid of The Great Stink solved the city's cholera problem. There was one more small outbreak in 1866, but it was in a neighborhood that was not yet connected to the sewer system. Once that system was complete, in 1875, London was safe from cholera—although it still kills tens of thousands of people in other parts of the world each year.

BRING OUT YOUR DEAD

Human waste isn't just poop and pee. It's also . . . well . . . humans.

Nobody likes to think of dead bodies as waste, but what do you do with them? If everyone who died, everywhere in the world, were buried in a coffin in a cemetery plot, we'd soon run out of space for anything else. That's the problem the French city of Paris faced in the 1700s. Its cemeteries were overflowing, and the smell of rotting corpses was overpowering in some neighborhoods. And still more people were living, dying, and being buried in Paris.

The Parisians turned to the Catacombs. Beneath the streets of Paris are hundreds of kilometers of tunnels,

In 2015, Arizona researchers reported finding treasure in sewage sludge. Based on what they found, they estimated that a year's worth of treated sewage from a city of a million people contains about $13 million worth of metal—$2.6 million of it silver and gold. They suspect the gold and silver get into the sewage through manufacturing processes, such as mining, electroplating, and the manufacture of jewelry.

GOLD

many of them abandoned mineshafts dating back 1,000 years or more. Starting in 1786, old graves in Paris's cemeteries were dug up, and the bones of the dead—all that was left of them—were moved into the Catacombs. It took 12 years to move the bones of more than 6 million dead people. Some had died as long as 1,200 years ago.

Today, all those bones have become a tourist attraction. You can visit the Catacombs of Paris and see millions of skulls and bones stacked neatly and respectfully along the walls of tunnels deep under the modern city.

The dead of Singapore aren't a tourist attraction. Most of them are ash. The island city faces an even bigger space problem than Paris did. There's really no room for the dead. At least, not for very long. You *can* bury a dead person in a cemetery in Singapore, but only for 15 years. After that, the body will be dug up, and what's left will be moved to a smaller space or cremated. Actually, almost two-thirds of Singapore's dead are cremated right away, without the 15-year wait. Families can keep the ashes at home or scatter them on the sea south of the city-state.

Trash Talk

Flying toilet

A bag of human poop flung out of a window. In informal settlements without sewage systems, many people use buckets or holes lined with plastic bags as toilets. Then they throw the bags into the street at night, when no one can see.

Gardyloo!

A warning cry formerly used in Edinburgh when throwing slops (liquid waste, including sewage) from upper-story windows into the streets.

GARDYLOO!

Honey wagon

A wagon or truck used to pump sewage out of pit toilets, portable toilets, holding tanks, and septic tanks, and carry it away for disposal.

Honey Wagon

PLUMBING the DEPTHS

For a century and a half, we've known how important it is to keep the stuff that comes out of us completely separated from the water that goes into us. For most people who live in wealthier countries, it's just a matter of flushing the toilet. One *whoosh* and the waste is gone, and we're pretty confident it won't end up in our drinking water to make us sick.

But about 2.5 billion people aren't that lucky, according to a 2014 World Health Organization report. They don't have good sewage systems—or, often, any sewage systems at all. And hundreds of millions of people have no access to safe drinking water. If you live in a country where clean water and indoor plumbing are common-place, this is hard to imagine. How can you poop and pee safely when there's nowhere to do it? And how can you wash your hands afterward if there's no clean water?

The 2 million people who live in 200 informal settlements in Kenya's largest city, Nairobi, face that problem daily. Such settlements are common in many parts of the world. People looking for work in the city simply build shacks and move in. The shacks and huts are almost always jammed close together, with no sewers and only a few pit toilets (basically holes in the ground).

BATHROOM

LAVATORY

REST-ROOM

WASHROOM

WC

Where do you go when you need to pee? In North America, you might go to the bathroom, even if the room has no tub. In Britain and parts of Europe, you might go to the W.C. (short for water closet). In an airport or shopping mall, you'd go to the restroom—even if it's not very restful. There are even more words for *toilet* than there are for *garbage*!

Plenty of clever people around the world are working on solutions to the sewage problem. In Kenya, for example, a company called Sanergy has designed what it calls the Fresh Life Toilet—a cheap, easy-to-clean public toilet. It's a small concrete cubicle, with a simple toilet that directs liquid and solid wastes into separate bins. If you use one, you'll be met by an operator who provides toilet paper, sawdust to sprinkle on the waste to control the smell, and soap and clean water to wash your hands. The whole setup costs about $350 and can be assembled in a day.

Fresh Life Toilets in public areas are run as small local businesses, owned and operated by people in the communities. The owners charge a small fee for using the toilet. Every day, Sanergy waste collectors remove the sealed bins and haul them away to become fertilizer for Kenyan farms.

Another solution is a portable household toilet that doesn't use water at all. It's simply a neat white box with a toilet seat on top and a sealable container inside. Instead of flushing, you sprinkle dry material on the poop to keep the smell down. When the toilets were tested in the Caribbean country of Haiti, the dry material was crushed peanut shells and sugarcane waste. A couple of times a week, the full containers are collected and replaced with empty ones, and the poop is hauled off to a composting facility to be turned into fertilizer.

SMART IDEA

Bottles for Water

In 2014, a group of high school students in Nairobi, Kenya, collected 10,000 plastic water bottles. It wasn't, as you might think, a fund-raising project. It was a water-raising project.

The bottles will be used to make a cheap, low-tech filtration system to turn wastewater into usable water for people who currently have to buy water and boil it, just to wash clothes and dishes safely. Filters are simply made from mesh bags filled with cut-up, shredded plastic bottles. The whole system is a little more complicated, but the raw materials are just bags and bottles—about 150,000 of them. Once the new system is working, several thousand people should have safe water for showers, laundry, and flushing toilets.

The high school students said collecting 10,000 bottles was easy. Kenyans don't trust their tap water, so they buy bottles of drinking water and toss the empty bottles anywhere and everywhere. Turning discarded water bottles into water-making bottles seems right!

the BUSINESS of GARBAGE

OPEN 24hrs

In the Sahara Desert, surrounded by sand as far as the eye can see, sits a huge island of rock, about one-fifth the size of Iceland. It's called Messak Settafet, and it might be the world's oldest example of a place where garbage created by large-scale mining and manufacturing has actually transformed the landscape.

Half a million years ago, before our own species of human evolved, people began mining stone and manufacturing stone tools here. The rock that makes up Messak Settafet is sandstone. If you know what you're doing, it's fairly easy to split the layers apart and chip away at an edge to sharpen the stone into a knife, a scraping tool, or any other handy-dandy convenience popular at the time.

Tool manufacturing at Messak Settafet went on for hundreds of thousands of years, and those unknown ancient manufacturers left their mark. The huge rock outcrop is dotted with shallow depressions, small quarries where people hacked out stone. And it's covered with waste from the manufacturing process—stone flakes and chips, half-formed tools, and discarded tools, all made from Messak Settafet sandstone. In a 2011 survey, archaeologists counted an average of 75 bits of tools and tool-making debris per square meter. In places, they said, the landscape is almost a carpet of tools.

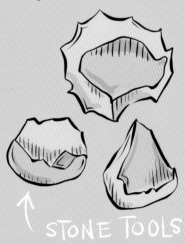

↑ STONE TOOLS

MININGTIP

DIGGING the DIRT

Messak Settafet might be the first example of a landscape changed by garbage, but it's not the last. Big business makes big garbage—and it always has. If you build with stone, for example, you have to dig out stone, cut it up, and leave the unusable bits behind. About 600 years ago, the Inca were building entire cities and roads of stone in South America's Andes Mountains.

The remains of the cities and roads are still there, and so are half-cut blocks of stone and broken tools, sitting in quarries or abandoned along old paths that linked the quarries to the building sites.

During the Industrial Revolution of the 18th and 19th centuries, big manufacturing got even bigger—and so did its waste. Coal powered the transportation systems and a lot of the mills and factories, so coal mining flourished. In Wales, which had plenty of coal, mines grew and so did the tips—piles of waste rock dug up with the coal. The tips were ugly, and sometimes they could be dangerous.

The village of Aberfan in southern Wales was built beside a coal mine that opened in 1869. By 1966, the village was dwarfed by seven huge tips. On October 21 of that year, the tip closest to the village began to slide downhill. Within a few minutes, 40,000 cubic meters (more than 1.4 million cubic feet) of rock—that's enough to fill 16 Olympic-sized swimming pools—had covered parts of the village, including the elementary school. Altogether, 144 people died, among them 116 children in the school.

COOL FACT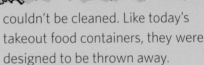

Olive Oil Built a Mountain

Olive oil was big business back in ancient Rome, and it produced its own kind of waste—Monte Testaccio. A big hill covered patchily with grass and bushes, it looms over a crowded neighborhood of trendy restaurants and shops. It looks like any other hill, but it isn't. Monte Testaccio is made entirely of broken amphorae, big pottery containers used 2,000 years ago to import olive oil. Archaeologists estimate the hill contains about 25 million of them.

The Romans imported oil by the shipload from other parts of the Mediterranean. When ships arrived, the olive oil was poured into large vats, and most of the amphorae were cleaned out and used again. But some couldn't be cleaned. Like today's takeout food containers, they were designed to be thrown away.

So, for 250 years, until 260 CE, the empty containers were smashed, then loaded on donkeys and hauled away to the growing heap of broken pottery that would become Monte Testaccio. Today, Monte Testaccio is just another of Rome's hills. Except, when you walk on it, you can hear the pottery fragments crunching beneath your feet. And you might come across archaeologists digging into the pile of broken pottery to learn more about the city's history.

BIGGER and BIGGER

Today, the garbage created by all kinds of businesses affects not just the land, but the air and the water. And it's quite different from the garbage that comes out of the average house or school.

Paper mills produce liquid waste that can poison the ground or water. Power plant chimneys spew out tiny particles of ash and clouds of carbon dioxide—both of which contribute to climate change. Piles of cinders mount up around factories that rely on heat

in the manufacturing process. Oil and gas wells release hydrogen sulfide gas, which smells like rotten eggs and can cause nasty health problems if you breathe too much of it.

Digging stuff out of the earth still produces garbage, too. Today's mines are a lot bigger than the Welsh coal mines of the Industrial Revolution, and they produce a lot more waste, or "tailings," as it's called in the industry. Usually, tailings consist of broken-up rock, chemicals used in the mining

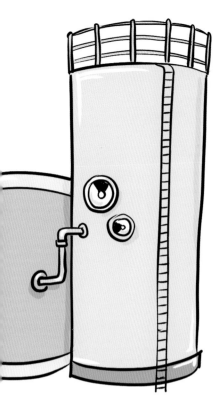

square kilometers (68 square miles), according to the Canadian Association of Petroleum Producers. That's twice the size of Manhattan Island in the heart of New York City.

The ponds are lined and dammed to keep the nasty stuff away from the surrounding environment, but that precaution doesn't always work. In another part of western Canada, the dam on a smaller tailings pond—just 4 square kilometers (1.5 square miles)—broke in 2014. The entire contents of the pond—both water and muck—poured into a small creek and on into a lake in the wilderness. The creek expanded from the width of a sidewalk to almost twice the width of a soccer field in a matter of minutes. There's a landscape change!

process, and contaminated water. Tailings are stored in huge ponds. At the Alberta oil sands in western Canada, tailings ponds cover 176

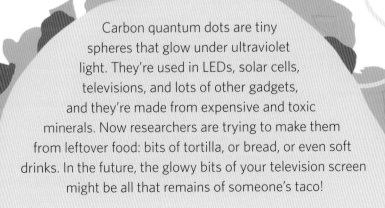

Carbon quantum dots are tiny spheres that glow under ultraviolet light. They're used in LEDs, solar cells, televisions, and lots of other gadgets, and they're made from expensive and toxic minerals. Now researchers are trying to make them from leftover food: bits of tortilla, or bread, or even soft drinks. In the future, the glowy bits of your television screen might be all that remains of someone's taco!

GROWING GARBAGE

Farming is a business, just like mining or manufacturing, and it creates its own set of wastes. Some are obvious. If you have a field full of cows, there's going to be plenty of manure. If your field is full of grain, you've got an awful lot of straw in your future. And a field of potatoes or tomatoes will leave unwanted greenery behind. All that stuff will rot away in time—but the rotting process releases methane, which increases global warming, and contaminants that can pollute local water supplies.

And then there's the plastic. Farmers use a surprising amount of the stuff. Bales of animal feed come wrapped in plastic sheets. Chemicals, fertilizer, and feed supplements come in plastic containers. Farms use plastic hoses, rope, tool handles, and greenhouses.

Growers of fruits and vegetables literally cover the ground with plastic—long strips of plastic film with just enough space left open for the crop to poke through. The plastic keeps weeds down and stops moisture from evaporating into the air.

If the plastic is dark, it absorbs heat from the sun and warms the ground, giving the crop a little more time to ripen. It helps keep us fed, but it also adds to the world's waste.

SMART PERSON

Candy Wrappers and Cigarette Butts

People throw stuff away because they don't know what else to do with it. What can you do with a chip bag, once the chips are gone? Or a candy wrapper, once you finish the candy? Tom Szaky will figure it out.

The Hungarian-born Szaky was attending university in the United States when he started thinking about ways to save all that wasted stuff. In 2001, he quit university and set up his own company, TerraCycle.

He started with worms. The worms turned garbage into compost, and TerraCycle sold the compost as liquid plant food,

packaged in used pop bottles. Today, the company operates in 25 countries—and it has moved way beyond worms. It makes flashy, reusable lunch bags and pencil cases from cookie and candy wrappers, turns juice pouches into paving stones, and recycles all kinds of plastic waste into the basic materials for new plastic products.

TerraCycle has even come up with a use for old cigarette butts. It transforms them into plastic shipping pallets. The leftover bits of tobacco are composted and turned into fertilizer—with help from the worms.

GARBAGE
—in—
BUSINESS

Business creates plenty of garbage, but garbage also creates business. There's money to be made in the collection and disposal of garbage, or in turning garbage into new products. In 2011, the United Nations estimated that the annual value of global waste-business activities, from collection to recy-

cling, was $410 billion. And that doesn't include the money generated by small-scale waste pickers who make a living collecting and recycling garbage in countries from India to Argentina.

That's an awful lot of money—enough to build almost three International Space Stations. Generally,

MARIO "STINKY" MALONE
— GARBAGE SHYSTER —

TONY "BABYFACE" BAMBINO
— TRASH STASHER —

the people involved in waste and recycling are doing an honest and worthwhile job, but that kind of money attracts dishonest people too. The most difficult stuff to get rid of is toxic waste, the sort of stuff that can pollute the land and water and make people sick or even kill them. And if you don't care much about the law or about hurting people, toxic waste can mean big money.

Most countries have strict laws about handling and treating toxic waste, but that treatment is often expensive, so some people look for a cheaper solution.

In Italy, at least since the early 1990s, the cheaper solution has been the Mafia, a famous criminal organization. Instead of paying a large amount of money to dispose of toxic waste safely, some businesses paid the Mafia less money simply to take the waste away. The Mafia just trucked the waste to rural areas in southern Italy and dumped it. Sometimes it was buried, sometimes it was left in a local dump, and sometimes it was simply discarded in a field, ditch, or canal. Some of those criminals were sent to jail, but the waste is still there. Now corroded drums leak liquid waste into the ground and water, piles of garbage catch fire and send plumes of poisonous smoke into the air, and open mounds of dangerous litter blow in the wind.

LEO "LEAKY" LATORRE
— RIVER POLLUTER —

ROSA "ROTTEN" RICOTTA
— REFUSE REMOVER —

BUSINESS
makes the WASTE go round

Waste doesn't always have to be a problem for businesses. Sometimes it's a solution. In Kalundborg, a small city in Denmark, there's an industrial park that creates very little waste. The waste products from one business become the raw materials for another.

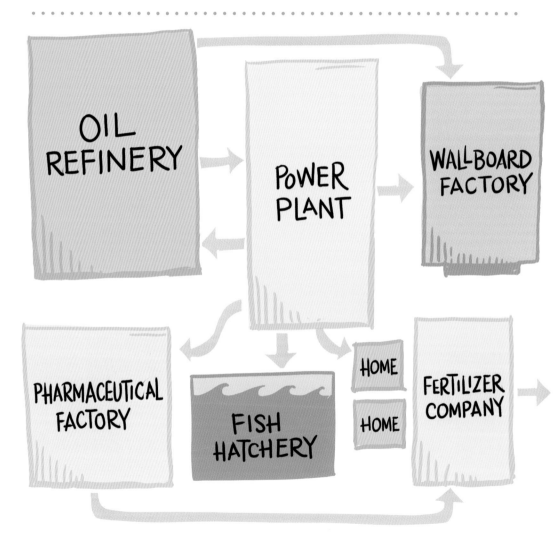

Wastewater from an oil refinery becomes cooling water for a power station. Waste steam from the power station helps run the refinery and a pharmaceutical plant. Waste heat from the power station warms local homes and a fish farm. Ash from the power station becomes the raw material for a wallboard factory, which is powered by waste gas from the oil refinery. Waste material from the pharmaceutical plant becomes fertilizer for local farms . . . and so on. The cycle now includes nine major businesses, as well as local homes and farms.

The Kalundborg eco-industrial park grew naturally, as businesses moved in and discovered that they could help each other—profitably. The local government saw what was happening and encouraged it. The city has even created a research institute to study efficient ways of reducing and reusing industrial waste.

Kalundborg isn't the only eco-industrial park, although it's one of the most successful so far. Others are located in Nova Scotia, Canada; Prato, Italy; Massachusetts, United States; and Lyon, France. The United Nations Environment Programme has even developed a handbook to help businesses and regions plan eco-industrial parks.

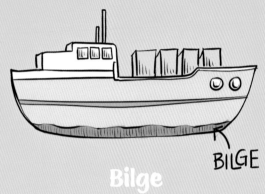

BILGE

Bilge

The lowest part of a ship, where dirty water (bilge water) collects, often contaminated with waste fuel or other dangerous substances. Bilge is also slang for something worthless.

Bobbins

English slang for useless junk. It probably comes from northern England, where hundreds of cotton mills shut down in the 20th century, leaving behind a lot of worthless machinery— including thousands upon thousands of bobbins, the basic tools in cotton milling.

CHAPTER 7

PROBLEM GARBAGE

There has always been garbage that didn't go away: think of those rock chips on Messak Settafet, or the shells scattered on an African cave floor. And there has always been dangerous garbage: think exploding dumps, collaps- ing tips, and leaking mine tailings. But in the last half-century, we've supersized our problem garbage production. For sticking around and causing trouble, it's hard to beat a couple of our newer inventions— plastic and electronics.

PLASTIC INVASION

Plastic waste is everywhere— blowing in the wind, tangled in bushes, and floating in the oceans. Especially floating in the oceans. In 2010 alone, according to a recent study, the amount of plastic that washed into the oceans was somewhere between 4.8 million and 12.7 million metric tons. And there's more plastic arriving every year.

It's hard to imagine, but 60 years ago the oceans were probably plastic-free. Plastic use didn't balloon until the late 1950s, and plastic shopping bags didn't even exist until 1965. Now, according to a 2014 United Nations report, each American uses an average of 1,200 plastic bags *a year*, as well as plastic toys, plastic dishes, plastic bottles, plastic yogurt containers, and all kinds of plastic packaging. People in Asia and Africa use less, but they're catching up fast.

Not much of that plastic gets recycled. The Worldwatch Institute's figures for 2012 show that in Europe, just over a quarter of plastic waste was recycled. About 36 percent was incinerated to produce energy, and the rest went to landfills. In the United States, only 9 percent was recycled in 2012. The rest—more than 30 million metric tons—was just thrown away.

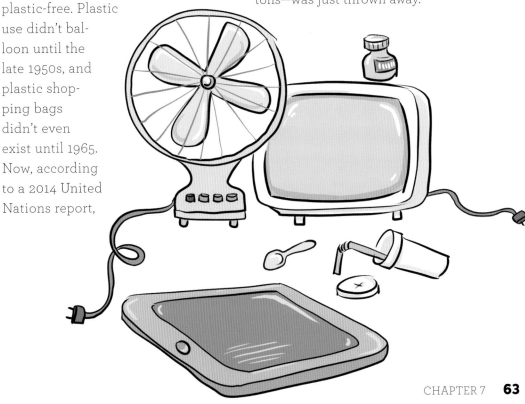

the GUEST who won't LEAVE

The biggest problem with plastic is that it doesn't go away. Ever, pretty much. Paper and wood and metal eventually rot or rust away. But plastic lingers. Nobody really knows how long, although some scientists estimate it could be as much as a million years. Think about that for a minute. If all the plastic in the world today is just a few decades old at most, it's going to be with us for a while—a long, long while.

Even our solutions to the plastic problem have turned out to be problems themselves. You can shred old plastic bottles and containers and turn them into cozy fleece jackets or blankets. We've done that, but now we know that those fleece jackets and blankets shed tiny plastic fibers every time they're washed. The fibers drain away into rivers and lakes and, eventually, into the ocean, where they join microbeads, the tiny bits of plastic put in face and body scrubs and some toothpastes. And plastic bags of all sizes and shapes. And old shampoo bottles, bits of plastic rope from fishing nets, plastic packaging, plastic coffee pods, and all kinds of bits and pieces of plastic garbage from almost every aspect of modern life.

In the oceans, the plastic bobs and drifts with the currents. Some of it washes up on beautiful beaches, far from its source. Much of it gets caught up in the oceans' five great gyres—the places where ocean currents meet and circle endlessly. The most famous of these sites has been called the Great Pacific Garbage Patch. There, the plastic bobs and floats, tangling around itself, trapping seabirds and whales, breaking into smaller pieces that fish and turtles swallow and even smaller pieces that make their way into every level of the ocean, right down to the seabed.

Nurdles

Tiny plastic pellets that are the first stage in making plastic products. They are shipped to factories in huge containers on trucks and trains. Some fall out of the containers to litter rail lines, where birds, insects, and small mammals can eat them.

Graywater

Wash water from sinks, showers, baths, washing machines—all the used water coming from a household, except toilet water. It can be reused for such purposes as toilet flushing or watering the garden.

GADGET
GARBAGE

There's a new kind of garbage on the block—even newer than plastic garbage. It's discarded electrical and electronic equipment, from washing machines to cell phones. Collectively, it's called e-waste, and it's a problem for several reasons: it's valuable, it's dangerous, and there's a lot of it. And as with plastic waste, governments and international agencies are struggling to find ways to deal with it.

Think of all the electronic or electrical gadgets in your house, including video game consoles and electronic toys. Then think about how often they break or become obsolete. Many of them can't be fixed or updated. Or maybe you don't want to repair that old television set or update the operating system on your old computer. You'd rather have a cool new TV or the latest tablet.

But you're a responsible person, so you take the old gadget to the recycling center, confident that you're doing the right thing.

Maybe. Maybe not.

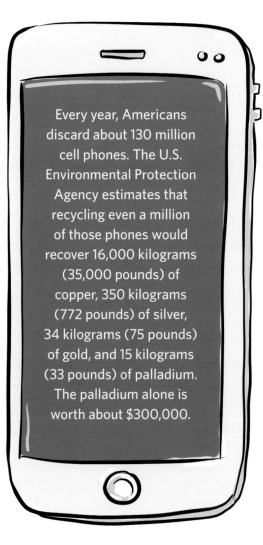

Every year, Americans discard about 130 million cell phones. The U.S. Environmental Protection Agency estimates that recycling even a million of those phones would recover 16,000 kilograms (35,000 pounds) of copper, 350 kilograms (772 pounds) of silver, 34 kilograms (75 pounds) of gold, and 15 kilograms (33 pounds) of palladium. The palladium alone is worth about $300,000.

THE LONG RECYCLING ROAD

Modern electronic gadgets are full of valuable materials—precious metals, such as gold, copper, and nickel, and rare materials, such as indium and palladium—that can be recovered and reused. But they are also full of dangerous materials, things that can seep into the environment and poison it. Mercury, lead, and cadmium, for example. Or brominated flame retardants. They're chemicals that are added to the plastics in electrical and electronic goods to reduce the chance of fire. But if they get free, they spread easily through water and food and make both people and animals sick.

The safe recycling of e-waste can be expensive. That's why there's a booming illegal trade. It's hard to track, and it's hard to stop. A truckload of old computers collected as e-waste in the United States, for example, might be bought by a dealer who labels them as secondhand goods and exports them to a country where there are fewer rules about recycling safely. And then, suddenly, they're e-waste again, about to be taken apart for their valuable components.

WHERE DOES IT END UP?

Ten years ago, a shipment of e-waste would likely have ended up in China. The region of Guiyu was the world center of illegal e-waste processing. People worked in their homes, taking old electronics apart, sorting out the valuable materials, burning away the plastic to get at the metals. None of it was done safely, and the consequences have been serious. Toxins from the electronic equipment leaked into Guiyu's soil, water, and air. From there, they got into the food people eat, and then into the people. Many children in Guiyu now have illnesses linked to the toxins.

China is trying to prevent more damage by shutting down its illegal e-waste business, and many other countries are scrambling to enact laws that will make e-waste recycling safer. More e-waste is now going to other Asian countries, such as Vietnam, India, and Bangladesh, where the law hasn't yet caught up with the problem. And more and more e-waste is going to Africa for the same reason.

Africa's largest e-waste dump—and one of the largest in the world—is in Accra, Ghana. About 20,000 people depend on the earnings of the dump's recyclers. The people who work at the dump, many of them children, are already experiencing health problems because of the toxic materials, but there might be help on the way. In the fall of 2014, two Ghanaian organizations teamed up with an international environmental group to turn the e-waste dump into an e-waste recycling center. They began by installing wire-stripping machines. That means the plastic can be stripped off the valuable metal wires without burning it and releasing toxic fumes. It's a long way from the goal of a full recycling center and healthy recyclers, but it's a start.

SMART IDEA

Trash Heroes in Paradise

Koh Lipe is one of Thailand's most beautiful islands, with white sand beaches, warm seas, and thick green jungles. And plastic garbage. Ocean currents bring floating garbage to Koh Lipe and the smaller islands surrounding it from as far away as India, Malaysia, and Myanmar.

In December 2013, a group of local residents decided to organize regular beach cleanups. They founded an organization called Trash Hero Thailand and started the tradition of Trash Hero Mondays.

Every Monday, a small flotilla of boats ferries volunteers—many of them tourists—to a remote beach. The volunteers spend a few hours picking up and bagging garbage. They enjoy a free lunch supplied by local businesses, have a swim in the sea, and then head back to Koh Lipe with full garbage bags. Most of the garbage goes to the mainland for recycling and processing, with the remainder headed to the local dump.

In the first 18 months, Trash Hero volunteers collected 80,000 flip-flops, 61,500 plastic bottles, 16,000 plastic lighters, 18,800 glass bottles, 200 cubic meters (7,063 cubic feet) of Styrofoam, and 3 tons of nonrecyclable waste. Several other Thai communities and at least one town in Indonesia have now started their own Trash Hero programs.

the FUTURE of GARBAGE

← HUMANS WERE HERE!

We've always had garbage to deal with, but now we have a garbage problem that's out of this world! We're actually leaving litter in space.

Several hundred thousand bits of space junk, from dead satellites to dropped tools and fragments of old rockets, are orbiting Earth. We've even left garbage on the moon—about 181 metric tons of it. That includes 5 American flags, 12 pairs of boots, a feather, some very expensive cameras, and 96 bags of pee, poop, and puke.

How do we clean up all of this space junk? That's a question scientists are still trying to answer. In the meantime, we have plenty to do right here on Earth. Fortunately, a lot of smart people are working hard to solve our garbage problem.

PLASTIC be gone

One of the most urgent problems we face is the amount of plastic waste thrown away each year. Plastic bags are a big part of the problem, especially flimsy single-use bags that go straight in the garbage. However, governments, businesses, and individuals are working on solutions.

Many stores, for example, now provide heavier bags that can be used again and again. And quite a few places—countries, states, cities, even individual stores—charge a small fee for plastic bags. The idea is to encourage people either to bring their own cloth bags or reuse the plastic bags. The charge helps to pay for disposing of the bags safely.

Other places have banned plastic bags entirely. In 2008, the small African country of Rwanda banned single-use bags. Business owners who violate the ban can spend a year in jail, and anyone caught carrying a bag can be fined. Border officers even search people's luggage at the airport to make sure they aren't bringing bags into the country. The result?

A huge reduction in the country's garbage problem and much cleaner, more pleasant streets in the capital city, Kigali. In fact, just months after the plastic bag ban went into effect, the UN declared Kigali the cleanest city in Africa. Several other African countries have now banned bags, and the idea is spreading.

Slowing the plastic waste stream is only half the battle. The other half is cleaning up the plastic already out there—especially those huge and dangerous garbage patches of plastic swirling around the ocean. A young Dutch man, Boyan Slat, might have a solution.

ABSOLUTELY, POSITIVELY NO PLASTIC BAGS! SERIOUSLY.

CLEAN OCEAN

HOLES TO DRAW
THE PLASTIC IN

FLOATING
BOOM

COLLECTED
PLASTIC

When he was still a university student, Slat came up with an idea: long, floating booms—log-shaped barriers—that would drift in the ocean gyres. The ocean currents would push plastic waste into the corral formed by the booms, and a solar-powered extraction platform would remove the plastic from the ocean. In 2013, Slat quit university and set up a foundation to make his idea a reality. A study conducted with the help of 100 volunteer scientists and engineers concluded that the system might well work, and efforts began to make it happen. The foundation's experts estimate that one 100-kilometer (62-mile) array of booms and extraction platforms could collect 42 percent of the plastic floating in the oceans in just 10 years.

WASTE-To-ENERGY

Sweden isn't any tidier than the rest of the world, but the Swedes might be a bit smarter. They're getting rid of their garbage—*and* making a profit. Swedish people produce their fair share of household garbage, but only a tiny portion of it ends up in landfills. As much as possible is reused or recycled. Most of the rest is turned into energy.

In waste-to-energy plants dotted around Sweden, garbage is fed into huge incinerators that burn it up. The heat turns water to steam, the steam spins generators to produce electricity, and the electricity flows back into the electrical grid to power the country's homes and businesses. The system works so well that Sweden now imports waste from several other countries and turns it too into electricity—for a fee.

And Sweden hasn't stopped at garbage. Sewage is being turned into energy, too. In Gothenburg, the country's second-largest city, the solid waste from city sewage is used to produce biogas, which is sold at local filling stations as fuel for cars. Gothenburg's energy company adds the heat produced by the treated sewage to its district heating network. Sewage heat provides inexpensive hot water and space heating for about 36,000 apartments in the city.

Sweden isn't alone in the waste-to-energy push—just ahead of the pack. Cities around the world are investing in waste-to-energy systems with the idea of getting rid of waste, reducing greenhouse gas emissions, and saving money, all at the same time.

SHRINKING the GARBAGE

The best solution to our garbage problem, of course, is no garbage. But that's unrealistic—garbage just happens, as part of living and using resources. We can, however, reduce the amount of unnecessary garbage we create. It just takes a little cleverness.

A couple of young women in Berlin, Germany, are fighting back against plastic bags, foil wrappers, cans, bottles, and all the other packaging that goes straight to the garbage. They've opened a small grocery store called Original Unverpackt (meaning, roughly, "Original Unpacked"). It has rows of neatly labeled glass jars and jugs, woven baskets, and clear plastic dispensers filled with a variety of foods. You can also buy toothpaste, laundry soap, and other household items. Shoppers bring their own containers or buy reusable ones at the store, fill them up, pay, and carry them home in their own shopping bags. When they need more of anything, they simply bring the containers back to be refilled.

We can't always get rid of packaging entirely. For example, we need protective packing material to ship breakable goods like computers or furniture. But how about making it out of mushrooms instead of plastic? An American company turns the threadlike filaments grown by fungi into shaped protective packaging that looks and acts like Styrofoam. The difference is that once you unpack your computer, you can crumble up the packaging and add it to the garden soil.

Freegans go beyond reducing and reusing packaging. They try to use everything and waste nothing. Freegans are people who believe we use too much of the world's resources, so they try to live from the things other people throw away, including clothing, furniture, and food. They patrol the

STYROFOAM VS.

MUSHROOMS

An elementary school in Ontario, Canada—St. Marguerite d'Youville in Hamilton—has managed to whittle its garbage down to a single bag each day. Everything else is recycled or composted, with some of the compost going into the school's butterfly garden. In 2015, St. Marguerite d'Youville shared the title of Greenest School in Canada.

alleys and collect food discarded by restaurants and food stores.

It sounds a bit disgusting, browsing through alleys and rooting through dumpsters to find your dinner. But there's a surprising amount of good food available if you know where to look. Most freegans know the best sources in their neighborhoods and the best times to check them. They also learn to share. If you find an entire case of cheese and half a bakery shelf of bread, you'd better have lots of friends who like cheese sandwiches!

NEW GARBAGE, NEW AWAY

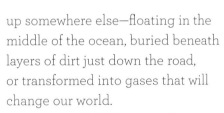

All of these ways of whittling down our global garbage pile go back to the two questions at the beginning of this book: What is garbage? And where is "away"?

Garbage is whatever we choose to declare garbage. Freegans choose to think that nothing is garbage and try to use it all. The Swedes take garbage and transform it into energy. The Rwandans and those two young women in Berlin try to avoid things that might become garbage.

And "away"? Well, there really is no away. The stuff we throw away simply turns

up somewhere else—floating in the middle of the ocean, buried beneath layers of dirt just down the road, or transformed into gases that will change our world.

But instead of letting garbage change our world, we can change the world of garbage. As we've seen, plenty of people are already working on the problem. We can all join them.

DISCARD DARE

Here's a dare: list all the things in your house or school that are designed to be thrown away. You can probably start with the plastic pen you use to write the list.

On second thought, it might be better to give yourself a time limit. Otherwise, this is going to be a very long list. So—how many things can you list in five minutes?

Want some hints? How about that plastic sandwich bag, the cardboard milk carton in the fridge, the foam takeout container in the garbage bin? Or plastic toys that can't be fixed when they break? Or a cell phone, discarded for something faster and fancier?

You could make this a class challenge. Who can come up with the longest list? And then, maybe you can figure out what to do about it. How about litterless lunches? Or giving up disposable plastic water bottles? Or . . . maybe you'll come up with an even better idea.

FURTHER READING

Burns, Loree Griffin. *Tracking Trash: Flotsam, Jetsam, and the Science of Ocean Motion.* HMH Books for Young Readers, reprint edition, 2010.

Kelsey, Elin. *Not Your Typical Book about the Environment.* Owlkids Books, 2010.

Mulder, Michelle. *Trash Talk: Moving Toward a Zero-Waste World.* Orca, 2015.

Newman, Patricia. *Plastic, Ahoy!: Investigating the Great Pacific Garbage Patch.* Millbrook Press, 2014.

Szaky, Tom, and Albe Zakes. *Make Garbage Great: The Terracycle Family Guide to a Zero-Waste Lifestyle.* Harper Design, 2015.

ONLINE RESOURCES

The Center for Green Schools: centerforgreenschools.org. Resources to help schools reduce their impact on the environment.

IFIXIT: ifixit.com. A website with free repair manuals and instructions for fixing all kinds of things, from tablets to teddy bears.

"Your Cool Facts and Tips on Waste Management": eschooltoday .com/waste-recycling/waste-management-tips-for-kids.html. Lots of information about what waste is and what kids can do about it.

SELECTED BIBLIOGRAPHY

Aguirre, Itziar. "Cairo's 'Zabaleen': A Rare Success Story." *International Policy Digest*, June 12, 2015. Retrieved June 18, 2015, from internationalpolicydigest.org/2015/06/12/cairo-s-zabaleen-a-rare-success-story/.

Anwar, Liyna. "Closing America's Largest Landfill, without Taking Out the Trash." NPR, February 22, 2014. Retrieved December 14, 2014, from npr.org/2014/02/22/280750148/closing-americas-largest-landfill-without-taking-out-the-trash.

Associated Press. "Too Much Human Faeces on Mount Everest, Says Nepal." *Guardian*, March 3, 2015, theguardian.com/world/2015/mar/03/too-much-human-poo-on-mount-everest-says-nepal.

Barbalace, Roberta C. "Plastics—From Recycling Bin to New Product." EnvironmentalChemistry.com, February 6, 2007. Retrieved February 26, 2015, from environmentalchemistry.com/yogi/environmental/200702plasticrecycling.html.

BBC Newsbeat. "Britain's Biggest 'Fatberg' Removed from London Sewer." August 6, 2013, bbc.co.uk/newsbeat/article/23586290/britains-biggest-fatberg-removed-from-london-sewer.

Berg, Nate. "With Urbanization Comes Mountains of Trash." *CityLab*, June 13, 2012. Retrieved September 9, 2015, from citylab.com/work/2012/06/urbanization-comes-mountains-trash/2273/.

Bland, Eric. "Island of Trash or the 'Garbage of Eden'?" *New Scientist*, April 12, 2007.

Borromeo, Leah. "Berlin Duo Launch a Supermarket with No Packaging." *Guardian*, September 16, 2014.

Brown, Louise. "'Father of the Blue Box' Died This Week." *Toronto Star*, February 4, 2011.

Campbell, Lise. "Real Junk Food Project: The Leeds Cafe That Has Fed 10,000 People, Using 20 Tonnes of Unwanted Food—and Started a Worldwide Movement." *Independent* [London], December 16, 2014.

CBC News. "Tailings Ponds for Mining and Oilsands Waste: FAQs." August 5, 2014, cbc.ca/news/technology/tailings-ponds-for-mining-and-oilsands-waste-faqs-1.2727889.

Chakraberty, Sumit. "From Waste Picker to Recycling Manager." *Citiscope*, April 14, 2014. Retrieved June 17, 2015, from citiscope.org/story/2014/waste-picker-recycling-manager.

Corkum, Kim. "10 Worst Examples of Packaging Waste." PLAN website, June 16, 2014. Retrieved November 8, 2015, from postlandfill.org/examples-of-packaging-waste/.

Crossland, Ian. "The World's First Ocean Cleaning System Will Be Deployed in 2016." *Minds* (blog), May 28, 2015. Retrieved June 1, 2015, from minds.com/blog/view/450715060952633344/the-world039s-first-ocean-cleaning-system-will-be-deployed-in-2016.

Daigle, Katy. "One-Third of World's People Still Have No Proper Toilets." Associated Press, June 30, 2015.

Dash, Mike. "Quite Likely the Worst Job Ever." Smithsonian.com, June 29, 2012. Retrieved April 22, 2015, from smithsonianmag.com/history/quite-likely-the-worst-job-ever-319843/.

DEQ Louisiana. "Did You Know . . . . Landfills" (information sheet). N.d. Retrieved September 22, 2014, from deq.louisiana.gov/portal/Portals/0/assistance/educate/DYK-Landfills.pdf.

Economist. "Oceans of Waste." February 19, 2015.

Electronics TakeBack Coalition. "Facts and Figures on E-Waste and Recycling." June 25, 2014. Retrieved June 24, 2015, from electronicstakeback.com/wp-content/uploads/Facts_and_Figures _on_EWaste_and_Recycling.pdf.

Ellen MacArthur Foundation website. "Kalundborg Symbiosis." ellenmacarthurfoundation.org /case-studies/effective-industrial-symbiosis.

Ellickson, Paul B. "The Evolution of the Supermarket Industry: From A&P to Walmart." *Handbook on the Economics of Retail and Distribution*, edited by Emek Basker, Edward Elgar Publishing, 2016, pp. 368–91.

Ezban, Michael. "The Trash Heap of History." *Places Journal*, May 2012.

Feltman, Rachel. "Half the World's Sea Turtles Have Eaten Plastic, Study Claims." *Toronto Star*, September 19, 2015.

Ferdman, Roberto A. "Americans Throw Out More Food Than Plastic, Paper, Metal, and Glass." *Washington Post*, September 23, 2014.

Figueiredo, Jordan. "Eating 'Ugly,' a New Healthy Trend." *Policy Innovations*, March 4, 2015.

Flegenheimer, Matt. "Wet Wipes Box Says Flush. New York's Sewer System Says Don't." *New York Times*, March 13, 2015.

Foley, Robert A., and Marta Mirazón. "Lithic Landscapes: Early Human Impact from Stone Tool Production on the Central Saharan Environment." *PLOS One*, March 11, 2015.

Food and Agriculture Organization of the United Nations. *Food Wastage Footprint: Impacts on Natural Resources; Summary Report.* 2013, fao.org/docrep/018/i3347e/i3347e.pdf.

Fredén, Jonas. "The Swedish Recycling Revolution." Sweden/Sverige website, updated September 24, 2015. Retrieved February 26, 2015, from sweden.se/nature/the-swedish-recycling-revolution/.

Friendly, Alfred. "Vindolanda." *Expedition* (Penn Museum), July 1975.

Geiling, Natasha. "Beneath Paris' City Streets, There's an Empire of Death Waiting for Tourists." Smithsonian.com, March 28, 2014, smithsonianmag.com/travel/paris-catacombs-180950160/.

Grossman, Elizabeth. "The Biggest Source of Plastic Trash You've Never Heard Of." Ensia, March 30, 2015. Retrieved March 30, 2015, from ensia.com/features/the-biggest-source-of-plastic-trash -youve-never-heard-of/.

Gustavsson, Jenny, Christel Cederberg, Ulf Sonesson, Robert van Otterdijk, and Alexandre Meybeck. *Global Food Losses and Food Waste: Extent, Causes and Prevention.* Food and Agriculture Organization of the United Nations, 2011.

Hitchings, Lauren. "Why Illinois Has Banned Exfoliating Face Washes." *New Scientist*, June 23, 2014.

Hoornweg, Daniel, and Perinaz Bhada-Tata. "Global Waste Management Practices." *What a Waste: A Global Review of Solid Waste Management*, Urban Development Series, Knowledge Papers, no. 15, Urban Development and Local Government Unit, World Bank, March 2012.

Hoornweg, Daniel, Perinaz Bhada-Tata, and Chris Kennedy. "Waste Production Must Peak This Century." *Nature*, October 31, 2013.

Hoornweg, Daniel, Philip Lam, and Manisha Chaudhry. *Waste Management in China: Issues and Recommendations*. Urban Development Working Papers, no. 9, East Asia Infrastructure Department, World Bank, May 2005.

Humes, Edward. *Garbology: Our Dirty Love Affair with Trash*. Avery, 2012.

IFIXIT website. ifixit.com.

Jefferies, Duncan. "50m Tonnes of E-waste Generated Every Year—and It Is Increasing." *Guardian*, April 2, 2014.

Jordan-Stanford, Rob. "These Dry Toilets Could Clean Up Haiti's Slums." *Futurity*, May 13, 2015. Retrieved October 5, 2015, from futurity.org/haiti-slums-toilets-919762/.

Kachur, Torah (interviewer). *What a Waste* (radio series). CBC Radio, 2014, cbc.ca/whatawaste/.

Kaplan, Matt. "Million-Year-Old Ash Hints at Origins of Cooking." *Nature*, April 2, 2012.

Kardish, Chris. "How Rwanda Became the World's Unlikely Leader in Plastic Bag Bans." *Governing*, May 2014. Retrieved October 10, 2015, from governing.com/topics/transportation-infrastructure/gov-rwanda-plastic-bag-ban.html.

Kashty, Meagan. "Loblaw's 'Ugly' Food Line Provides Big Savings." *MoneySense*, March 13, 2015. Retrieved March 14, 2015, from moneysense.ca/spend/loblaws-ugly-food-line-provides-big-grocery-savings/.

Khan, Saifullah. "Sanitation and Wastewater Technologies in Harappa/Indus Valley Civilization (ca. 2600-1900 BC)." *Evolution of Sanitation and Wastewater Technologies through the Centuries*, edited by Andreas N. Angelakis and Joan B. Rose, International Water Association, 2014.

Kongrut, Anchalee. "Cleaning Up the Accolades." *Bangkok Post*, June 22, 2015.

Larsen, Janet, and Savina Venkova. "The Downfall of the Plastic Bag: A Global Picture." Earth Policy Institute website, May 1, 2014. Retrieved June 21, 2015, from earth-policy.org/plan_b_updates/2014/update123.

Leschin-Hoar, Clare. "Fleeced Again: How Microplastic Causes Macro Problems for the Ocean." *Grist*, December 7, 2011.

Lewsey, Fred. "Saharan 'Carpet of Tools' Is the Earliest Known Man-Made Landscape." University of Cambridge *Research News*, March 11, 2015. Retrieved April 30, 2015, from cam.ac.uk/research/news/saharan-carpet-of-tools-is-the-earliest-known-man-made-landscape.

Lin, Jiaoqiao, Na Lin, Liming Qiao, Jie Zheng, and Chi-Chung Tsao. "Municipal Solid Waste Management in China." Unpublished academic paper, January 2007.

Lobell, Jarrett A. "Sorting through a Mountain of Pottery to Track the Roman Oil Trade." *Archaeology*, n.d. Retrieved April 17, 2015, from archaeology.org/exclusives/articles/2892-rome-monte-testaccio-amphoras.

Loomis, Ilima. "Air Force Turns a Keen Eye on Space Junk." *Science*, January 9, 2015.

Lovett, Richard A. "Huge Garbage Patch Found in Atlantic Too." *National Geographic News*, March 2, 2010.

Lu, Vanessa. "TerraCycle Turns Trash into Goods, Thanks to Volunteers, Companies." *Toronto Star*, June 19, 2013.

Lum, Zi-Ann. "99 Per Cent of Sweden's Garbage Is Now Recycled" (video). *Huffington Post Canada*, September 2, 2014, huffingtonpost.ca/2014/09/02/sweden-recycling_n_5738602.html.

Matheson, Rob. "The Surprising Value of Waste." *MIT News*, February 14, 2014.

Messenger, Stephen. "Everglades Islands Are Actually Ancient Piles of Trash." *Treehugger*, March 21, 2011. Retrieved April 3, 2015, from treehugger.com/natural-sciences/everglades-islands-are-actually-ancient-piles-of-trash.html.

Modak, Prasad (chapter coordinating author). "Waste: Investing in Energy and Resource Efficiency." In *Towards a Green Economy: Pathways to Sustainable Development and Poverty Eradication*, United Nations Environment Programme, 2011, pp. 287–330. unep.org/greeneconomy.

Morris, Eric. "From Horse Power to Horsepower." *Access*, Spring 2007.

Nagle, Robin. "Material Remains: The Perpetual Challenge of Garbage." *Scientific American*, October 25, 2013.

National Oceanic and Atmospheric Administration Marine Debris Program. *2014 Report on the Occurrence and Health Effects of Anthropogenic Debris Ingested by Marine Organisms*. National Oceanic and Atmospheric Administration, 2014.

Nuwer, Rachel. "Are There Any Pollution-Free Places Left on Earth?" *BBC Future*, November 4, 2014.

Owano, Nancy. "Sweden Wants Norway's Trash (and Lots of It)." *PhysOrg*, October 28, 2012.

Parker, Laura. "Eight Million Tons of Plastic Dumped in Ocean Every Year." *National Geographic News*, February 13, 2015.

Penaluna, Regan. "This Floating Contraption Could Scoop Out Absurd Amounts of Ocean Plastic." *Nautilus*, November 6, 2015, nautil.us/blog/this-floating-contraption-could-scoop-out-absurd-amounts-of-ocean-plastic.

Petru, Alexis. "A Brief History of the Plastic Bag." *Triple Pundit*, November 5, 2014. Retrieved June 21, 2015, from triplepundit.com/2014/11/brief-history-plastic-bag/.

Rathje, W. L. "The Garbage Project & 'The Archaeology of Us.'" Originally appeared as "The Archaeology of Us," *Encyclopaedia Britannica's Yearbook of Science and the Future—1997*, edited by C. Ciegelski, Encyclopaedia Britannica, 1996, pp. 158–77. Retrieved November 4, 2014, from humanitieslab.stanford.edu/23/174.

Royte, Elizabeth. *Garbage Land: On the Secret Trail of Trash*. Little, Brown, 2005.

Ryan, Jacob. "Turning Trash into Treasure: Massive Trash Site 'Hiriya' Turns into Israel's Largest Eco-park." *NoCamels: Israeli Innovation News*, February 19, 2015. Retrieved June 29, 2015, from nocamels.com/2015/02/landfill-site-hiriya-ariel-sharon-park-recycling/.

Salter, Stephen. "Inspiration from Sweden." Georgia Strait Alliance website, n.d. Retrieved November 7, 2015, from georgiastrait.org/inspiration-from-sweden/.

"Sanergy." Kiva website, n.d. Retrieved April 26, 2015, from kiva.org/partners/258.

Schiller, Jakob. "Inside the Hellscape Where Our Computers Go to Die." *WIRED*, April 23, 2015. Retrieved April 23, 2015, from wired.com/2015/04/kevin-mcelvaney-agbogbloshie/.

Sedghi, Ami. "How Much Water Is Needed to Produce Food and How Much Do We Waste?" *Guardian*, January 10, 2013.

Singh, Timon. "19-Year-Old Develops Ocean Cleanup Array That Could Remove 7,250,000 Tons of Plastic from the World's Oceans." *Inhabitat*, March 26, 2013.

Skidelsky, William. "The Freegans' Creed: Waste Not, Want Not." *Observer*, July 19, 2009.

"Space Surveillance and Tracking—SST Segment." European Space Agency website, updated February 11, 2014. Retrieved February 26, 2015, from esa.int/Our_Activities/Operations/Space_Situational _Awareness/Space_Surveillance_and_Tracking_-_SST_Segment.

Spooner, Samantha. "Africa Has an Astonishing Food Waste Problem—This Is What One Group Is Doing about It." *Mail and Guardian Africa*, December 17, 2014.

Steinfeld, Carol, and David Del Porto. *Reusing the Resource: Adventures in Ecological Wastewater Recycling*. Ecowater Books, 2007.

Stromberg, Joseph. "When Will We Hit Peak Garbage?" Smithsonian.com, October 30, 2013. Retrieved June 23, 2015, from smithsonianmag.com/science-nature/when-will-we-hit-peak -garbage-7074398/.

Stuart, Tristram. *Waste: Uncovering the Global Food Scandal*. W.W. Norton, 2009.

Sykes, Tim. "Mushroom-Based Packaging Becomes a Reality." *Packaging Europe*, January 10, 2014, packagingeurope.com/Packaging-Europe-News/60424/MushroomBased-Packaging-Becomes -a-Reality.html.

United Nations Department of Economic and Social Affairs. "World Population Projected to Reach 9.7 Billion by 2050." July 29, 2015. Retrieved October 2, 2015, from un.org/development/desa/en /news/population/2015-report.html.

Urbina, Ian. "Disco Rice, and Other Trash Talk." *New York Times*, July 31, 2004.

Vindolanda Tablets Online (website). vindolanda.csad.ox.ac.uk.

Waymouth, Belinda. "Eco-Minded Kids + Water Filtration in African Slum = Ingenious Reincarnation of Plastic Bottles." *Huffington Post*, March 19, 2015, huffingtonpost.com/belinda-waymouth /ecominded-kids-water-filtration-in-african-slum_b_6899280.html.

Wilson, David C. (editor in chief). *Global Waste Management Outlook*. United Nations Environment Programme, 2015.

Yardley, Jim. "A Mafia Legacy Taints the Earth in Southern Italy." *New York Times*, January 29, 2014.

Young, Emma. "Garbage Betrays Date of Earliest Village Life." *New Scientist*, November 16, 2004.

Zimring, Carl A., and William L. Rathje. *Encyclopedia of Consumption and Waste: The Social Science of Garbage*. SAGE, 2012.

ACKNOWLEDGMENTS

This book was very much
a partnership with Annick
Press. My thanks to
everyone there, especially to
Linda Pruessen, Paula Ayer,
and Colleen MacMillan.

—CE

INDEX

Claire Eamer grew up in the middle of the prairies and now lives in the middle of the ocean. (Well, on a coastal island in British Columbia, Canada—but it's really quite oceany.) In between, she has lived at the edge of the Arctic and in a large European city. She is sorry to say that she has produced garbage in all of these places, but she's trying to cut back.

Claire is fascinated by all things scientific, and her books on science have won a number of awards and honors, including the 2013 Lane Anderson Award for a Canadian youth science book.

Bambi Edlund lives with a big fluffy dog and a small bossy cat in Vancouver, BC. She loves that her job is to draw all day, and she can't resist slipping rats into her illustrations whenever possible. She grew up in the country, and she went on regular trips to the garbage dump with her dad. She hated the smell but loved the huge ravens that seemed to sit on every old washer, empty barrel, and pile of tires in the place.

If you liked *What a Waste!* check out these other books by Claire Eamer:

Before the World Was Ready: Stories of Daring Genius in Science

Claire Eamer, illustrated by Sa Boothroyd
paperback $14.95 | hardcover $24.95

*Lane Anderson Award winner
*Red Cedar Book Award finalist
*2015 Information Book Award finalist

"This engaging book has much to offer both children and adults and would be a wonderful personal gift or addition to any science classroom or library."
—*The Guardian*

The World in Your Lunch Box: The Wacky History and Weird Science of Everyday Foods

Claire Eamer, illustrated by Sa Boothroyd
paperback $14.95 | hardcover $22.95

*Eureka! Children's Book Award, Silver
*Next Generation Indie Book Award
*Red Cedar Book Award

"With a kid-friendly structure and super-goofy illustrations, this is probably the best book on the history and science of familiar food to have been published for kids in recent years."—*School Library Journal*